T0010102

DIVA LEGENDS ALPHABET

Words by Robin Feiner

A is for **A**dele.
'Hello, it's me.' One of the most relatable artists for her emotion-filled songs, the Queen of Hearts speaks her mind and tells it like it is. With a focus on equal rights for all and a body-positive attitude, Adele empowers women everywhere by making 'music for ears, not eyes.'

B is for Barbra Streisand. Whether strutting her stuff in the studio or on the stage or screen, Babs owns them all. As an artist, she insists on full creative control. As a strong female role model, she shows the world that beauty is much more than skin deep. It's no surprise she was awarded the Presidential Medal of Freedom.

C is for Mariah Carey.
In her own Cinderella story, Mariah drew attention when she handed her demo tape to a record executive, who then spent two weeks searching for her. With her five-octave voice, this legend has earned 19 number-one hits, including 'All I Want for Christmas Is You'—the biggest holiday song ever!

D is for Celine Dion.
When her manager discovered 12-year-old Celine, he was so sure of her talent he used his own money to back the start of her career. Dion went on to win five Grammys, become the singer of Titanic's famed 'My Heart Will Go On,' and continues to astonish with her soulful voice.

E is for Gloria Estefan. '1-2-3-4. Come on, baby, say you love me!' The Queen of Latin Pop left the streets of Havana for the shores of Miami to rock America with infectious conga beats. In 1995, Gloria became the first pop star ever to perform for the Pope. A true diva legend.

Ff

F is for Aretha Franklin.
The first woman ever inducted
into the Rock and Roll Hall of
Fame, Aretha blazed the path
for every female artist who
followed. Hits including 'Think'
and 'Chain of Fools' landed the
Queen of Soul more songs on
the charts than any other
female. 'R-E-S-P-E-C-T'

G is for Lady **G**aga. Known for her musical diversity and edgy artistic expression, it's no surprise that Mother Monster was influenced by Madonna and Bowie. In a bold act of protest, she once wore a dress made of meat to an MTV awards show. No wonder we're all gaga about this lady.

H is for Billie **H**oliday. Considered one of the greatest jazz singers of all time, Lady Day could make it up on the spot. Her unmistakable personal style was also present in the songs she wrote, among them, 'God Bless the Child' and 'Lady Sings the Blues.' The echo of her influence can still be heard throughout the jazz world.

I is for Idina Menzel.
As Elphaba in Wicked, Idina earned devoted fans with her iconic voice and dramatic flair. As the voice of Elsa in Disney's Frozen, she inspires: '... the fears that once controlled me can't get to me at all. It's time to see what I can do.' And so she does. Superbly!

J is for **J**anet Jackson. The youngest member of the famous Jackson family recorded her first album when she was just 16, scoring three hit singles. Ever since, she's been a passionate influencer in dance-pop music and a woman with a message— that music can unite the people of the world to overcome injustice.

K is for Kylie Minogue. After blazing her way to international stardom doing 'The Loco-Motion,' this Australian pop sensation proved she was no singing budgie by churning out countless chart-topping hits. 'Get outta my way, got no more to say.' Sit up and pay your respects, world.

L is for Cyndi Lauper.
This legend caught the world's attention with her eccentric style and distinctive, crystal voice. From 'Girls Just Want to Have Fun,' her anthem of female independence, to the accepting embrace of 'True Colors,' Lauper hits just the right notes to make us love her back.

M is for Madonna.
Madge, the Queen of Pop,
the Material Girl—whatever
you call her, this legendary
singing and dancing diva has
proven she's here to stay.
A feminist, style, and business
icon, too, they don't come
bigger and more influential
than Madonna.

N is for Stevie **N**icks. With Fleetwood Mac and her stellar solo career, Stevie and her legendary talent are always on full display. Considered the most important female voice in rock music, she was the first woman to be inducted into the Rock and Roll Hall of Fame twice.

O is for **O**livia Newton-John. This innocent and lovable Australian might have won four Grammys, but it was her electrifying role in the musical Grease that set the world alight. She started out singing country, but Olivia left all that behind, becoming a pop diva with the smash hit 'Physical.'

P is for **P!nk**
With awe-inspiring acrobatics and a my-way-or-the-highway attitude, P!nk flaunts her one-of-a-kind sound and message. A role model for women and girls everywhere, she reminds them that no one else should define them: 'What happened to the dream of a girl president?'

Q is for 'Queen Bey' Beyoncé Knowles. Competing on Star Search at the age of 12, Queen Bey's group lost the competition, but she's more than made up for it. With a record number of Grammys for a female artist, this diva uses her platform to encourage and empower women. 'Run the World (Girls)'!

R is for Diana **R**oss. Named the most successful female music artist in history by the Guinness Book of World Records, Diana over-came every social and musical divide that stood between her and the worldwide stage. Powerful and ambitious, she proves there 'ain't no mountain high enough' to stand in her way.

S is for Britney Spears. The '...Baby One More Time' sensation blazed her way onto the music scene over twenty years ago, redefining pop while she was at it. With her signature breathy voice and edgy moves, Brit-Brit delivers her hits and continues to forge a fierce and independent path.

T is for **T**ina Turner.
Taking control of any stage,
Tina struts her trademark
legs and swirling mane of
hair to claim her title as Queen
of Rock and Roll. This legend
smashed all the boundaries
for female and black artists
to reign supreme while
demanding, 'You better
be good to me'!

U is for Carrie Underwood. Winner of American Idol's fourth season, this country queen is the show's most successful contestant ever. Whether she's singing her latest country hit, a rock classic, or gospel song, Carrie nails them all. Inducted into the Grand Ole Opry and holding eight Grammys, Carrie proves her star's still rising!

V is for Christine McVei. This legendary singer, songwriter, and Rock and Roll Hall of Fame inductee is famous as one of Fleetwood Mac's lead singers. Counting some of the band's biggest hits as hers, including 'Little Lies', it's no rumour that many believe the real voice of the band was McVei.

W is for Whitney Houston. The Voice is considered one of the best vocalists of all time. Whitney's signature song, 'I Will Always Love You,' is one of the best-selling singles ever, while her perfect pitch assures we will always love her. Legendary.

X is for Xtina Aguilera. 'Nobody can hold us down, never can, never will.' Strut and swagger and a voice full of riffs and runs are this legend's trademarks. Never afraid to experiment, Christina has dabbled in pop, R&B, hip-hop, rock, and soul and created her alternate persona, Xtina, sporting black hair and tattoos.

Yy

Y is for Yolanda Adams. Once a teacher hoping for a modeling career, the First Lady of Modern Gospel found her true calling in music. With her own blend of jazz, contemporary urban, hip-hop, and traditional gospel, this diva's music has a special message.

Z is for Jane **Z**hang.
This artist made music history when 'Dust My Shoulders Off' became the first song by a Chinese artist to make the US digital download charts. Unwilling to settle for just one, she followed up with another chart-maker—'808.' A rising international star, Jane sings in Chinese, English, and Spanish.

The ever-expanding legendary library

DIVA LEGENDS ALPHABET
www.alphabetlegends.com

Published by Alphabet Legends Pty Ltd in 2022
Created by Beck Feiner
Copyright © Alphabet Legends Pty Ltd 2022

Printed and bound in China.

9780645487084

The right of Beck Feiner to be identified as the author
and illustrator of this work has been asserted by her in
accordance with the Copyright Amendment (Moral Rights)
Act 2000.

This work is copyright. Apart from any use as permitted
under the Copyright Act 1968, no part may be reproduced,
copied, scanned, stored in a retrieval system, recorded or
transmitted, in any form or by any means, without the prior
permission of the publisher.

This book is not officially endorsed by the people and
characters depicted.

ALPHABET LEGENDS